do MOOSE ever...?

Fran Hodgkins
Photographs by Paul Cyr

Down East Books
Camden, Maine

Down East Books

Published by Down East Books
An imprint of Globe Pequot
Trade division of The Rowman & Littlefield Publishing Group, Inc.
4501 Forbes Blvd., Ste. 200
Lanham, MD 20706
www.rowman.com
www.downeastbooks.com

Distributed by NATIONAL BOOK NETWORK

Designed by Lynda Chilton, Chilton Creative

Copyright © 2022 by Fran Hodgkins

Photographs copyright © Paul Cyr, except pgs 2 (pudu) public domain, 5 (elk) public domain, 9 (antler velvet) Walter Siegmund, 21 (orcas) Robert Pittman/NOAA

ISBN 978-1-60893-736-3 Hardcover
ISBN 978-1-60893-737-0 E-book

Printed in Malaysia (June 2022)

Have you ever met a moose?

You've probably seen them in cartoons and TV shows, depicted as big, goofy deer (maybe with a flying squirrel sidekick.) Moose are big. Moose are deer.

But goofy?

Read on to find out more about moose!

What is a moose?

A moose is the largest member of the deer family. Deer are part of a very large group of mammals that includes animals with cloven, or two-part, hooves. Other mammals in this group include cattle, pigs, sheep, goats, and giraffes.

The smallest species of deer is the pudu, which stands just a foot high when an adult. The largest, of course, is the moose.

Deer live naturally all over the world, except in Antarctica and Australia, though they've been introduced to Australia.

Is there just one kind of moose?

There's just one species of moose, *Alces alces*. (Some scientists think American and European moose are different, but we'll just go with the one.) *Alces* is a Latin word that means "elk." So a moose is an "Elk elk."

When you're talking about moose, remember: one *moose*, two *moose*. Moose is one of those words in English that doesn't change to a plural form. No mooses, no meese. Just moose.

How did they get the name "moose" anyway?

The word *moose* came to English from the Algonquin language, spoken by the Innu people of Quebec, Canada. It means "stripper and eater of bark."

Why do scientists use Latin names? Because local names can be confusing. For example, people in Canada and the United States call the moose *moose*. In Europe, the same animal is called an *elk*. But to North Americans, an *elk* is a different animal altogether!

Do male and female moose look different?

You bet! All moose have long legs, strong bodies, humped shoulders, and large heads. Adult females weigh between 600 and 1,200 pounds, and males range from about 800 to 1,400 pounds. In North America, male moose are about 11 feet long, and females, about 10 feet; their European relatives are smaller, about 7 to 9 feet long.

Moose are *TALL*! On average, moose measure between 6 and 7 feet tall, though some sources say that the biggest moose can reach nine feet at the shoulder. To picture just how big that is, think of your house or apartment. Most likely, the height of each room measures about eight feet. A moose would not fit into your house. Which makes hiding one in your bedroom very difficult.

Their front legs are longer than their back legs, which lets them jump over fallen trees easily.

Bulls are dark brown, and cows and calves are usually lighter colored. Unlike other deer, moose have square upper lips that hang over their lower lips, and a flap of skin, called a bell, hanging from their necks, which is smaller in the cows.

Their hooves are big, too. A moose track is heart-shaped, with the point of the heart pointing forward, and about five to seven inches long.

How many moose are there?

In many parts of the United States, moose were once rare because they had been overhunted. However, they've made a comeback. In the United States, most moose live in Alaska, which has about 175,000; followed by Maine, which has about 75,000 moose. Sweden has the densest population of moose in the world, with 350,000 animals.

Antlers

Each year, male moose grow broad antlers that can be as much as six feet wide from tip to tip. Unlike deer antlers, which are branched like a tree, moose antlers have a flattened part that tines stick out from. The antler looks a little bit like an open hand—the flat part is the palm and the tines are fingers.

Moose, like nearly all other deer, grow new antlers every year. They grow from spots on the top of the head called the pedicle. The bone of the antler grows out of the pedicle. As it grows, it is covered by a soft layer of skin called velvet. The velvet is rich with blood vessels that nourish the growing antler. While the antlers are in this velvet stage, they can be easily damaged.

When the antlers are done growing, both the velvet and the bone of the antler die. The moose rubs the velvet off the antlers, using trees and bushes. The antlers are now ready for use!

WHAT ARE ANTLERS?

Antlers are bony growths that are on the heads of most kinds of deer (some deer have tusks instead). They aren't part of the animal's skull like horns are. Cattle, antelope, goats, and sheep have horns. Antlers are made of bone.

How do moose use their antlers?

Male moose use their antlers to push each other around. When breeding season arrives in the fall, the males compete for the right to mate with females. Battles between males involve lowering those massive antlers and shoving for all they're worth. The way the antlers are shaped provide built-in eye protection for the bulls.

Sometimes the antlers get locked together, and the bulls are unable to get free. In 2007, rangers at Denali National Park in Alaska found the skulls and antlers of two huge bulls that had died in this way; they're now displayed at one of the park's visitor centers.

In December, the moose shed their antlers, losing about 60 pounds as they do!

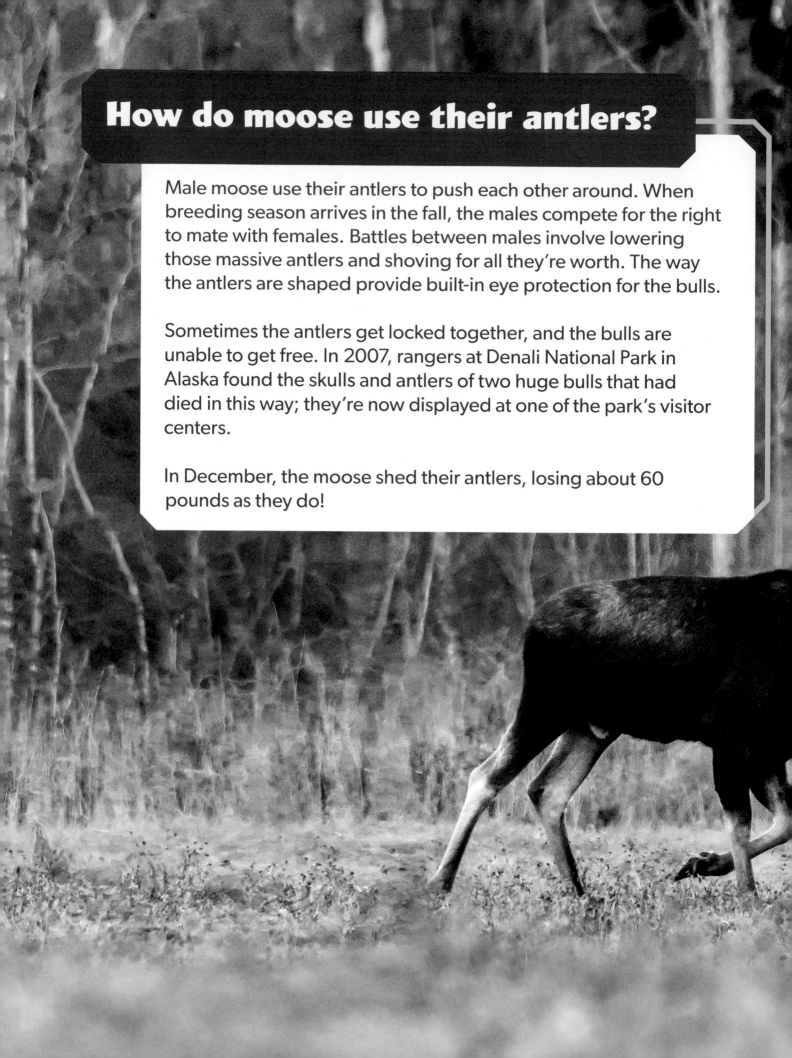

Do moose have homes?

Moose don't have a lodge like a beaver or a den like a bear. Instead, they have a home range. A home range is an area in which the moose will wander, browsing as it goes.

Do moose live in herds?

Herd animals follow a leader. Moose are individualists. They prefer to live solitary lives. Males and females will connect during mating season, and sometimes moose can be found together in a spot with especially delicious food. Female moose and their babies, or calves, live together for about a year.

How do moose sleep?

Like horses, moose often sleep standing up. They may lean against a tree, close their eyes, and relax their head and neck. Yet while they sleep, their ears are on the alert for any hint of danger.

Sometimes, moose prefer to lie down to sleep. They may tuck their legs underneath them. Or, they may stretch out on their side. This may be uncomfortable for a moose with a big rack of antlers, but somehow, they manage.

Getting up involves tucking the legs under, raising the hind end first, and then the front end.

How many babies does a moose have at a time?

Most of the time, moose give birth to one baby, or calf. There are exceptions, though, and moose twins are pretty common (and cute!). Once in a great while, when the conditions are just right, a moose may have three calves.

What does a baby moose look like?

Moose calves are cinnamon colored. They have long legs, even by moose standards, and big eyes. They don't have those big noses, though, or antlers. They can walk the first day they are born, and in a couple of weeks they can even swim.

Whether a solo, duo, or trio, the babies stay with mom for at least a year and a half, longer if the calf is female. Youngsters nurse for about five months and grow quickly on the cow's rich milk. Even after they no longer nurse, young moose will stay with mom for protection.

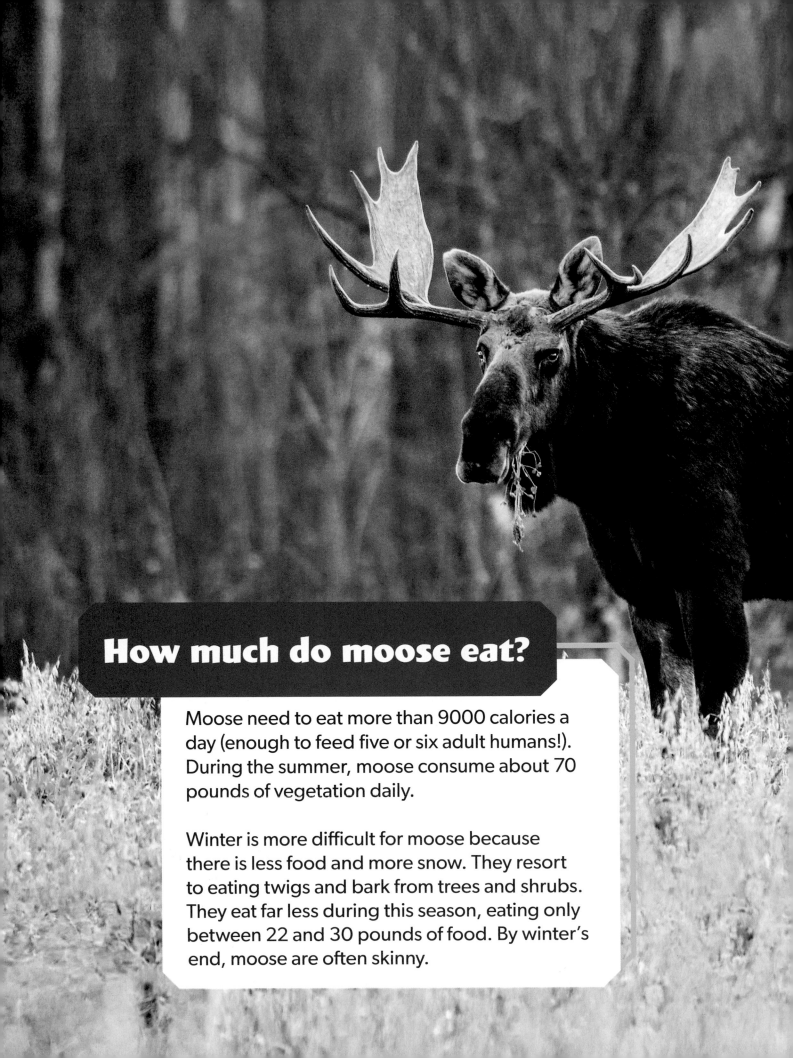

How much do moose eat?

Moose need to eat more than 9000 calories a day (enough to feed five or six adult humans!). During the summer, moose consume about 70 pounds of vegetation daily.

Winter is more difficult for moose because there is less food and more snow. They resort to eating twigs and bark from trees and shrubs. They eat far less during this season, eating only between 22 and 30 pounds of food. By winter's end, moose are often skinny.

What do moose eat?

Scientists call moose *browsers*. Remember how the Innu called them "strippers and eaters of bark?" Yep, that's what's on the menu. During the winter, bark and twigs make up most of what moose eat. During the summer, they also eat leaves and will wade into ponds and lakes to get water plants, such as lilies, pulling up the plant root and all. To get these delicacies, moose are helped by their upper lips. Moose can stay underwater for more than 30 seconds.

Their favorite foods are willow and aspen trees, blueberry bushes, mountain ash, and buckthorn. They can also eat plants that are toxic, such as a grass called red fescue. Within this grass lives a kind of fungus that makes a toxin. Animals that eat too much of this toxin can lose their hooves! But scientists have found that the moose's spit contains a chemical that affects the fungus and cuts down on the toxin, which lets them eat the grass that would injure or kill another animal.

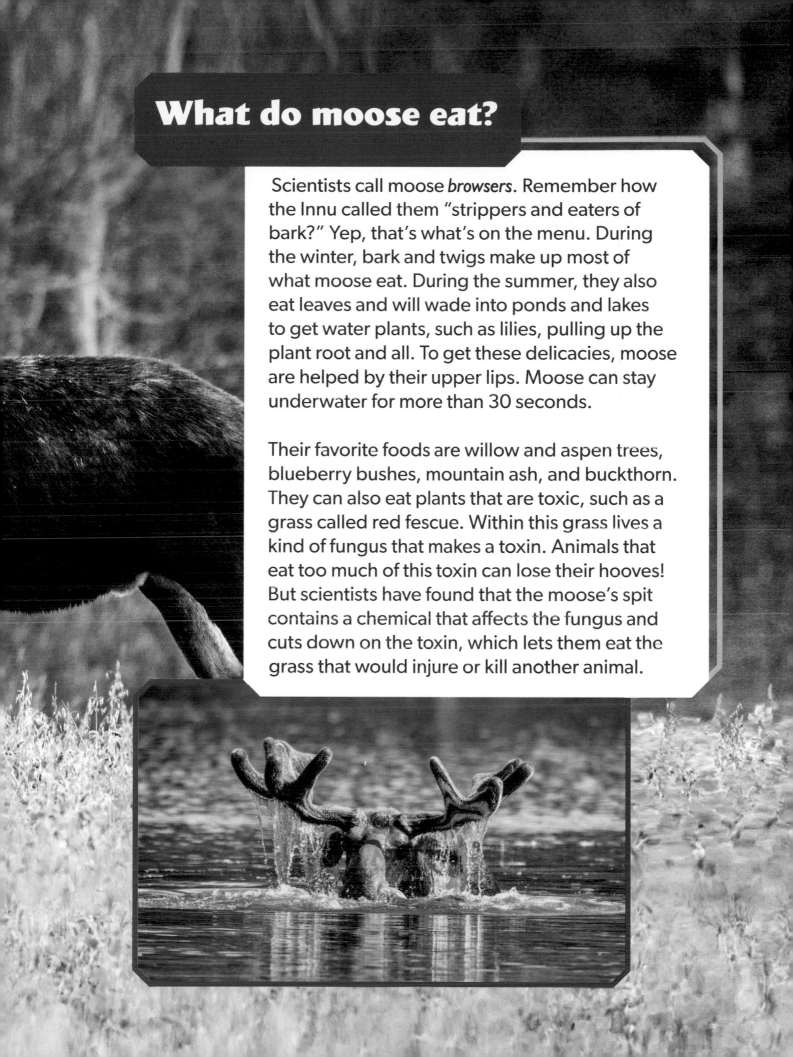

Do moose have good eyesight?

It depends on what you mean by good. People have good eyesight, but our eyesight is terrible when compared to a falcon's. White-tailed deer have been found to have eyesight that is perfect for detecting movement in their habitat, because they watch for predators like wolves and cougars. However, scientists haven't studied whether or not the moose's eyesight is similar. We do know that moose tend to have trouble seeing things that are far away.

However, that doesn't mean that it's easy to sneak up on a moose (that's not a good idea).

Moose have excellent hearing and an outstanding sense of smell. Those large noses contain millions of scent-sensitive nerve endings. Their noses and ears keep them well informed about their surroundings.

What do moose have to be afraid of?

An adult moose is bigger than most other animals in their habitat, but that doesn't mean they have nothing to fear. They can be preyed on by gray wolves, brown bears, black bears, coyotes, and mountain lions. In Russia, Siberian tigers prey on moose as well. Calves are most at risk, but a mom moose will fight fiercely to defend her baby, and a well-placed kick can kill a predator.

Humans are also among the moose's predators.

Believe it or not, killer whales are among the moose's predators, too! In the Pacific Northwest, moose sometimes swim between islands. Although moose aren't normally on the menu for this ocean predator, if an orca finds a swimming moose, it may attack. Well-equipped to protect itself from land predators, the moose has little way to defend itself in the water.

Can moose be tamed?

Officially, it's not recommended.

However, there have been stories of orphaned calves being raised on farms. One orphaned calf in Lithuania, for example, was saved by a farmer. After she grew up and returned to the wild, she would still come back to visit. There are also stories of moose being ridden and used to pull wagons and sleighs.

In 1900, Carnation the Moose pulled a sulky cart through the streets of Skagway, Alaska, scaring horses as he did so. Two other moose were trained to pull a similar cart in Seattle. And a team of trained moose pulled a cart at the Caribou, Maine, Winter Carnival in February 1942.

https://www.mainememory.net/artifact/9595/

How long do moose live?

Moose live between 7 and 15 years, though some can reach the age of 20.

How is climate change affecting moose?

Like all living things, changing climate is affecting moose. Because winters are less harsh than in the past, moose don't get a break from parasites. Previously, the ticks would jump off in April, hit the snow, and die. With less cold and snow, that isn't happening. Scientists are finding moose that are struggling to survive because they have so many ticks. Ticks attach themselves and suck blood from their hosts. Too many ticks and an animal will lose too much blood. Some moose have been found with as many as 75,000 ticks.

As they try to rid themselves of these parasites, the moose rub against trees so hard and so much that they wear their fur off. They are called "ghost moose." There may be other factors, but scientists aren't sure yet.

In Alaska, the changing climate has altered the land and its plants. Areas that had once been home only to the short plants of the tundra are now home to tree and shrubs like willows. Moose have followed the spread of the trees and shrubs into areas that had been home only to caribou. While the new range may be good for the moose, it's probably not good for the caribou.

Are moose dangerous to people?

Moose are usually pretty docile and peace-loving, but like any other wild animal, they can be dangerous if people are being dumb.

Females who are protecting their calves will try to trot away from people, but they can kick hard enough to kill a wolf or bear. Male moose have not only the kick, but the antlers—and during mating season, short tempers—so moose are best admired from a distance.

Those long legs aren't just dangerous for the kicks they can dish out. They are so long that they hold the moose's body about four feet off the ground, and out of the range of car headlights. Every year in Maine, more than 1000 traffic accidents involve moose and cars. These accidents are much more likely to be fatal for the driver than a collision with a deer.

I see a moose! What should I do?

Keep your distance! Moose aren't afraid of people, so you may be tempted to walk up and touch a moose that you encounter. No, no, and again, do not.

A moose may show you that you're getting too close for its comfort in several ways. First, it may stare at you. Hard. Worse than an "I can't believe you said that" stare.

If the stare isn't enough to make you back away (slowly), the moose may put its ears back while the hair along its neck, hips, or rump stand up. It might then lick its lips or clack its teeth.

If you are not on your way by that point, the moose will be more direct. It will lower its head and walk toward you. Remember, moose are as fast and as big as horses, while you are, well, as slow and as small as a human being. If the moose charges, you aren't going to be able to run faster than it can. And you aren't going to be able to outmuscle it, either.

However, if you are still pushing your luck, the moose may urinate and open its eyes wide so you can see the white part (the sclera). Finally, it may toss its head like a horse.

Of course, the moose may give no warning at all before charging.

It's best not to test a moose. They are bigger, stronger, and faster. Stay away.

What does the moose do for the forest?

Moose are what scientists call a "keystone species." Imagine an archway made of stones. At the top of the arch is one stone that keeps all the others steady and in place. That's the keystone. In its habitat, the moose has a huge impact.

First, they poop a lot. One study in Sweden calculated that moose add 300,000 tons of poop to the landscape each year. That may sound gross, but it's good for the plants because moose poop (like cow poop and horse poop) contains nutrients that are good for the soil.

Second, moose influence plants of the forest and how they grow—which has a big influence on the forest's biodiversity (variety of living things). Biodiverse forests are healthy forests.

So, you can see that moose are more than just cartoony goofballs. They're important to the survival of other animals (not just their predators), and even to the forest itself. Next time you see a moose, say thanks—softly, and from a safe distance, of course!